The Last Supper

A Maundy Thursday Portrayal

Susan E. Bartlett

and

Diana S. Smith

CSS Publishing Company, Inc., Lima, Ohio

THE LAST SUPPER

Copyright © 2001 by
CSS Publishing Company, Inc.
Lima, Ohio

For more information about CSS Publishing Company resources, visit our website at www.csspub.com.

ISBN 0-7880-1792-6

We dedicate this book to
John H. Tietjen, Th.D.,
Pastor of Trinity Lutheran Church,
Fort Worth, Texas.

Without his assistance, encouragement, and faith,
this work could never have been produced.

The Last Supper
A Maundy Thursday Portrayal

Note: This portrayal is written to be performed in the round. It was originally done following a Maundy Thursday congregational supper in the church's fellowship hall. The room was arranged to accommodate the meal and the portrayal. Tables were arranged in a hollow square, with seating on both sides. An elevated stage was in the center of the square. There was a small altar at one end of the room, prepared with the communion articles in keeping with the traditions of the congregation.

Characters:
Presiding Minister
Householder
Jesus
Mary
12 Disciples
(*See page 17 for a synopsis of each character*)

Setting: The Upper Room. A low, rectangular table, surrounded by large pillows for seating. There are candles on the table which provide most of the light. At one end of the stage are a small bench and a large basin. There are no actors on stage; the Presiding Minister speaks from the area near the altar. (*See page 21 for a seating chart for the Last Supper*)

Presiding Minister: Grace be unto you, and peace, from God our Father and our Lord and Savior, Jesus Christ. We have gathered here tonight to witness the last evening Jesus spent with his disciples before his crucifixion, and to relive with them the birth of the sacrament of Holy Communion.

(*PM moves to the altar to begin the service*)

PM: On every Lord's Day when we come together for Holy Communion, we remember that event. We do so, trusting his promise to be with us through his body and blood given for us. I will remind you now of what Jesus said and did so that through this bread and wine Jesus may be present for us tonight.

(*Words of Institution may be adapted to the practices of the denomination*)

PM: Jesus took the bread, gave thanks, and gave it to his disciples, saying, "Take and eat, this is my body given for you." In the same manner, also, he took the cup, gave thanks, and gave it to them, saying, "This cup is the new testament in my blood, shed for you for the forgiveness of your sins." (*Takes the bread and chalice of wine and places it on the table on the stage. As he/she places it on the table he/she says ...*) It all happened the night Jesus was betrayed. (*Leaves the stage and returns to the altar*)

Householder: (*Has entered from the opposite end of the room*) ... The night Jesus was betrayed ... I can tell you something about that night. No, I wasn't one of the chosen; I wasn't even a Christian ... then. But it all happened in my house. In the room above my living quarters. Some men, strangers to me, came earlier that day to inquire about renting a room. It was common knowledge in the city that I had a room for hire and that my daughter and I were accommodating hosts. The men wanted to make arrangements to have the room prepared for the Passover meal. Their master had sent them, they said. "And just who *is* your master?" I asked. With the Romans occupying the country, it was worth my life to be cautious. They told me he was Jesus of Nazareth. Now, I had never seen the man, but some of my neighbors had, and the tales they told were frankly hard to believe. Out of curiosity I consented to host the meal — with the agreement that there would be *no* trouble. I remember it as though it were yesterday ... they started to arrive a little before sunset ...

6

(*As Householder speaks, Peter and John enter with Judas, who goes to the Householder, removes money from a leather pouch on his belt, and pays for the use of the room*)

Peter: (*Looks over the semi-prepared room*) Does our master *ever* cease to amaze you, John? "Go to the city," he says, "follow a man carrying a water jar. Enter the house he enters. There you will find a room for our Passover meal. Make the arrangements." And look! Just as he said!

(*Judas approaches the two men*)

Peter: Judas, did you pay the householder?

Judas: I've taken care of my business.

John: Did you make the Passover donation?

Judas: Not yet. Jesus will be here soon. I'll take the money after I dine.

(*James and Andrew enter*)

Peter: Ahh, and here are my brother and yours, John ... Andrew! (*Hugs Andrew; John and James embrace*) James, how is it with your father?

James: Zebedee is well, but still ranting about the defection of his sons and best fishermen! Who knows why? The business isn't suffering!

Peter: And Andrew, have you brought no one new to meet the master?

Andrew: No, Peter, tonight it should just be family!

(The men pantomime a conversation while the Householder speaks. Judas is with them but stands just a little apart, does not attempt to converse, only listens)

HH: Those men, the four talking together, Peter, Andrew, James and John, all Galileans, all fishermen from Bethsaida. Some say that James and Andrew were at the water with John the Baptizer when he first set eyes on the Messiah, and that Andrew, too, could see that this was not just an ordinary man. He was the first, they say, to follow Jesus, and it was he who brought his brother, and James and John. And the other man, the one who paid me, Judas Iscariot, he was a leather-smith before he met Jesus, from Judea. The *only* Judean in the group.

(Philip and Bartholomew enter — each arrival is greeted with an embrace)

Peter: Philip! Bartholomew! Welcome! How does it feel, Philip, not to be in charge of the dinner preparations?

Philip: Highly unusual. But for a small group such as this, it would have been a pleasure.

Bartholomew: For Philip, anything less than 5,000 is no challenge!

(Matthew enters, carrying a parchment and pen. Simon is right behind him — there are greetings from the assembled)

Simon: We were very nearly late! The streets are jammed with people. Too many Romans! Is our master not here? Is he out there all alone?

Matthew: I have seen many of my old associates; not all of them were anxious to greet me!

Bartholomew: Maybe they don't recognize you outside of your tax office! You have changed more than a little since you joined us.

Matthew: It seems like several lifetimes since then. You're right, my friend, I hardly recognize myself.

John: Jesus should have been here by now. Who else are we missing?

Peter: Thaddeus. Thomas. And where is *your* brother, Matthew?

Matthew: I think I hear James and the others now.

(*James son of Alphaeus, Thaddeus, and Thomas enter — all exchange greetings and break off into small groups to converse in pantomime*)

HH: Such a diverse group of men — fishermen, tax collectors, scholars, but all with the same air about them. As if they knew something I didn't ...

(*Mary enters with a large jug of water and towels. She stops by James A., and as is the custom when a guest enters a house, invites him to sit on the bench and remove his sandals*)

Mary: Please, sir, may I remove the dust of the streets from your feet? (*Prepares to wash James' feet*)

HH: ... and the last to arrive was Jesus ...

(*Jesus enters the room, greets each man warmly by name, then moves to Mary's side*)

Jesus: Please. (*He gently raises Mary to her feet, removes his outer garment, takes the cloth from her hand, and begins to wash the feet of each disciple in turn*)

(*While Jesus washes, Mary leaves the room and returns with the traditional Passover dishes. As Jesus washes the feet of his disciples, the congregation sings an appropriate hymn. Suggestion: "Jesu, Jesu" affords the right amount of time*)

HH: (*As the singing ends and the foot washing continues*) Such an unbelievable gesture! Such a man of contradictions! Less than a week ago, hailed as a king! Now, washing the feet of his men in my very house! Ahh, but we were living in strange times. Strange and turbulent. Roman rulers, Roman taxes, all making for very anti-Roman sentiment. Israelite revolts! Some wanting only to live in peace with Rome, some wanting nothing short of complete freedom from Rome. It was hard to know which side to stay with. And then, this man, this Jesus, came into our midst. From where? For what purpose? Even his followers seemed divided on those questions. Some, like Simon, were Zealots, revolutionaries. They seemed to think Jesus would free the nation from Rome. Some, like Bartholomew, saw a much different kind of power in the man. A man of peace. A Messiah. Even *I* could feel that because of this man, our world would never be the same.

(*As he speaks, Jesus completes the washing of all but Peter's feet. Peter is obviously uncomfortable*)

Jesus: Peter? (*Motions for Peter to sit on the bench*)

Peter: Lord, are you going to wash my feet?

Jesus: You do not realize what I am doing, but later you will understand.

Peter: You shall never wash *my* feet.

Jesus: Unless I wash you, you have no part in me.

Peter: Then, Lord, not just my feet but my hands and head as well.

Jesus: A person who has had a bath needs only to wash his feet. His whole body is clean. And you are clean, though not every one of you.

(Peter acquiesces and takes his place on the bench, and Jesus completes the foot washing. Mary returns to remove the basin, pitcher, and towels. Peter helps Jesus put his robe back on)

Jesus: It is sunset. Let us begin the Passover meal. *(Leads the way to the table and takes his place at the center. Most of the disciples assume their places, John to the right of Jesus, the others in random order, but Peter and Judas both move to the left side of Jesus)*

Judas: This is *my* place at the table, Peter, as it has always been.

Peter: Judas, I will take the seat beside our master. It is *I* who have been with him the longest.

Jesus: Judas! Peter! Why do you two bother to argue over who is the most important? Have you never heard me say that the oldest among you should be like the youngest, and the one who rules, like the one who serves?

(Judas makes no move to back down, so Peter continues the argument)

Peter: But it is *I* who he relies on and can count on. Is that not so, Jesus?

Jesus: Peter, before the cock crows this night, you will three times deny that you even *know* me.

(Peter is speechless. Shakes his head in denial of Jesus' statement, but moves to the far end of the table in humility)

James A.: Teacher, why did you not let the woman wash our feet? That is the work of a servant.

Jesus: You call me "teacher," James? Have I not just taught the lesson that I have come to teach? You are to do for one another what I have done for you — serve one another, care for one another, love one another. Now, let us begin the meal.

(*Jesus prepares the ritual unleavened bread with bitter herbs, dips it into the charosheth, and offers the first sop to Judas. It is then passed to John and on around the table, each man breaking off his portion and dipping it in the paste. Then the lamb is passed around and the feast begins in earnest. While they eat, they pantomime a lively conversation*)

HH: Witnessing the meal that night was like watching a large, happy family at a holiday feast. There was much loud talking and laughter. They covered many topics. The past ...

Thaddeus: (*Has been staring at Jesus, then turns to Matthew*) Have I told you, Matthew, that I was there when our master was born?

Matthew: How was that, Thaddeus, you are hardly older than he is?

Thaddeus: I was only little! I was with some shepherds, just an errand boy for them really, but we went to the stable where he was born. Such a night! Such a beautiful little baby. I held him, you know! I followed every bit of news about him and then one day ...

Matthew: *He* found *you*! Amazing! He found me, too, in my tax office! As if some great sign was hanging over me saying, "Here is a man who really needs you, take him!" (*They laugh and continue on in pantomime*)

HH: The present ...

Thomas: I am still amazed by our master's reception here on Sunday. If I hadn't seen it with my own eyes, I wouldn't have believed it!

Philip: (*Shakes his head in agreement and turns to Bartholomew*) So, Bartholomew, do you still believe that the scriptures were right, that no good thing comes out of Nazareth?

Bartholomew: (*Laughs*) Stop taunting me with my own words, Philip! I am ever grateful that you didn't just leave me under that fig tree, but sometimes I wish you didn't have such a good memory for the past!

HH: The future ...

Simon: (*To James A.*) After Sunday, I see no reason why Jesus *couldn't* become governor or king or whatever he wants to be. The people love him! We need to be ruled by one of our own! Enough of Rome! (*Simon slams his fist on the table. James is silent but obviously agrees with Simon's sentiments*)

Thomas: What's next for us, Jesus? Where will you have us go when we leave here?

Mary: (*Joining her father*) Then the mood of the evening changed. It was as if a great sadness descended on Jesus ...

HH: And settled over all at the table.

Jesus: We will not always be together as we are this night. Soon I will have to leave you.

Peter: Where are you going? I'll follow you, wherever it is!

Jesus: You can't follow me right now, Peter, but you can later. All of you! Trust in God. And trust in me. In my Father's house there are many rooms, and I go to prepare a place for you.

Thomas: But, Jesus, we don't know where you're going! We don't know the way.

Jesus: *I* am the way, Thomas, and the truth, and the life. No one can come to my Father except through me. I'll come back and take you with me. Then we can be together yet again.

Philip: Lord, show us the Father and we will be satisfied.

Jesus: Have I been with you so long and yet you do not know me, Philip? He who has seen *me* has seen the Father. Before long, the world will not see me anymore, but you will see me.

Thaddeus: But, Lord, why do you intend to show yourself to us, and not to the world?

Jesus: If a man loves me, he will keep my word; and my Father will love him, and we will come to him and make our home with him.

Simon: We will keep your word; you can depend on all of us!

Jesus: I am telling you now, before it happens, that one of you will betray me.

(*The disciples all look at each other in disbelief. There is a great deal of head shaking and gesturing around the table. During the chaos, while the attention of the men is diverted, Jesus leans over to Judas and speaks. The audience can hear but the other men do not appear to*)

Jesus: What you must do, do quickly.

(*Judas very quietly rises and leaves the room, apparently unnoticed*)

Peter: John! Ask him who it is!

John: Who is it, Lord?

Jesus: One who has broken bread with me, John. But, my brothers, let not your hearts be troubled. Believe that what I do, I do for you.

Bartholomew: But what are we to do without you, Master?

Jesus: As you have learned to do in all times of uncertainty, pray to our Heavenly Father for help and guidance.

PM: Let us pray as Jesus prayed with his disciples ... (*Leads the congregation in the Lord's Prayer*)

Matthew: We will be lost without you.

Jesus: Oh, Matthew, all of you ... I will never be far from you.

(*Jesus stares at a yet untouched loaf of bread on the table, slowly picks it up, and holds it in front of him. The disciples watch him silently*)

Jesus: This is my body ...

(*Jesus breaks the bread into many pieces takes one piece, and passes the basket to John, who passes it to the next man, and on around*)

Jesus: ... Given for you ... Take and eat ...

(*After the men have eaten, Jesus raises the chalice, takes a drink, and passes it to John*)

Jesus: Take this and drink. This is my blood, which is shed for you and for everyone for the forgiveness of sins. When you eat and drink in this manner, we will be together even though we are apart. Remember — I will be with you always, even unto the ends of the earth.

(*The chalice is passed from man to man. One by one, the men rise from the table, seven of the disciples receive the plates of bread at the altar and begin to distribute the bread to the congregation. After the last man drinks, the remaining five disciples and Jesus go to the PM to receive the trays of wine. The PM joins them in the distribution of the wine. The HH and his daughter may assist if needed. After the communion is over, they remain standing with Jesus below the stage)*

Jesus: Now, my brothers, my peace I give to you. My peace I leave with you. Not as the world finds peace but only as our Father in heaven knows peace.

(Jesus and the disciples share the sign of peace, then share peace with the congregation)

Jesus: The time has come. Will you pray with me in the garden?

(Jesus leads the disciples out of the hall and to the sanctuary)

PM: Shall we follow him to Gethsemane? *(The congregation is led to the sanctuary while a hymn is played quietly)*

(The church is dimly lit except for the light in the chancel. Jesus is kneeling alone before the altar. The disciples are kneeling at the rail. All are in prayer. A soloist sings "Come To Dark Gethsemane." After the congregation is seated and the hymn ends, the disciples slowly rise, one or two at a time, to remove all objects from the altar. They do not return. When the altar is bare and he is alone, Jesus looks up)

Jesus: Father, if you are willing, take this cup from me. *(A bell tolls)* Yet, not my will, but thine, be done. *(The bell continues to toll slowly as the HH and his daughter usher the congregation out. Jesus is left alone in prayer. As the last person leaves, the church is darkened and the bell is silenced)*

Character Synopsis

Andrew: an evangelist known for his friendliness and his zeal for bringing men to meet Christ. He was Peter's brother. Andrew was at the water with John (the Baptist) and James when John first saw Jesus. He was probably the first to be called by Jesus, and was instrumental in bringing Peter to Jesus. Although he was the first, he was overshadowed by his flamboyant brother, a fact which didn't seem to bother him at all. Andrew was there to learn and to serve, just to be near Jesus.

Bartholomew: a searcher of scriptures and a seeker of truth. Unlike many of the disciples who followed Jesus because they believed that through him Israel could be politically free of Rome, Bartholomew was ardently seeking the Messiah as foretold by the ancient prophets. He was a man of meditation and prayer. In his studies, he found there was no mention of any great prophets coming out of Nazareth. He was, therefore, very disappointed when Philip wanted to introduce him to Jesus of Nazareth. Bartholomew couldn't believe that this could be *the* Messiah. He approached his meeting with Jesus openly skeptical, which led Jesus to say of him, "Here is one in whom there is no guile." Bartholomew was convinced very quickly that Jesus was Lord, when Jesus referred to knowing him before Philip called to him under the fig tree. Bartholomew had been studying about the Messiah, under a tree, when Philip came to bring him news of Jesus.

James son of Alphaeus: His mother was one of the Marys who stood by the cross when Jesus was crucified. There is the possibility that James and Matthew are brothers. His stature was small, and at times he was referred to as "James the Less" (John's brother James was a large man) but he much preferred the "son of Alphaeus" title. James loved Jesus very much and was so stricken by his death that he vowed not to eat or drink until he saw Jesus again in the flesh. Jesus appeared to him before he appeared to the others (James was growing smaller and weaker as the days passed) and James broke his fast by receiving bread and wine again from the hand of the Lord.

Matthew: a tax collector, not a very popular person due to the fact that the money he collected went to Rome! Taxes were levied on everything, including the use of roads, so the collectors usually had offices along major roadways. The benefit to being a tax collector was that it was acceptable to collect the requisite amount plus whatever amount *you* wanted to, and you kept the overage. He may have been the brother of James son of Alphaeus. Matthew was fairly well to do. He was able to use a pen and was probably the first to write a gospel. His life was empty and friendless however, and he spent hours in his office pouring over scripture, looking for meaning to his existence. He heard of Jesus through all the people passing by, exchanging gossip in his office, and felt that this might be what he was looking for. He invited a lot of his friends to dine with Jesus. This set Jesus up for criticism. Jesus sought Matthew out to be an apostle, probably because the need for spirituality in his life was so great that he would make a wonderful disciple.

Peter: a fisherman from the town of Bethsaida. He worked with his brother Andrew, and John and James, whose father owned the business. Apparently it was a successful venture; they had the best equipment and fished the deepest water. Peter was brought to Jesus by Andrew. He quickly became one of the inner circle with Andrew, James, and John. Peter was a flamboyant character — definitely an extrovert who spoke before he thought and often had to change his position later. He was typical of most Galileans in that he was a bit of an insurrectionist. Peter, in spite of his disavowal, was fiercely loyal to Jesus.

Philip: a fisherman. He was a realist, and faith without proof was hard for him. However, he was something of a natural evangelist. His best find was Nathaniel. He also brought a group of Greeks to meet and talk with Jesus. It appears that Philip was in charge of procuring food for the group, a real problem at the Sermon on the Mount!

Simon: a Zealot. Zealots were ultrapatriotic, intensely religious people dedicated to restoring divine rule in Israel. They were violent revolutionaries, guerrilla fighters, feared by the Romans as well as any Jews who tried to cooperate with Rome. Like many of the apostles, Simon believed that following Jesus was a way to a political end. Jesus endeavored not to take sides with the Jews against Rome or with Rome against the Jews. He did, instead, choose followers from the various factions. After his death and resurrection, even the nationalistic apostles understood what Jesus was here to do.

Thaddeus: As a very young boy, he was with a group of shepherds who were inexplicably led to a stable in Bethlehem. He was so entranced by the beauty of the mother and newborn baby in the stable that he stayed after the shepherds returned to the field. The baby's mother let Thaddeus hold the child. This established a life-long bond between them. Thaddeus followed Jesus' career until he was called by Jesus to join him. As an adult, Thaddeus, like many of the apostles, became a violent nationalist. Some of the scholars believe that Jesus' followers were with him because they believed that he was the way to freedom from Rome and not necessarily a heavenly Messiah. It wasn't until after the resurrection that they all grasped the true reason for Jesus' presence among them.

Thomas: Many people confuse realism with permission, and concrete thinking with doubting. Because of this, Thomas has been given a bad reputation. Thomas was with Jesus when word came about the death of Lazarus. Thomas' response was, "Let us go and die with him." This wasn't pessimism, as twice in the previous four months the Jews had threatened to stone Jesus, and there was a fair amount of anti-Jesus sentiment in Bethany, where Lazarus lived. The "Doubting Thomas" label was stuck on him because he *needed* to see and touch Jesus' wounds before he could believe it was him. Although Thomas at times seemed melancholy or doubtful, he was a solid, reliable apostle who was willing to follow our Lord even into death.

Judas: Thank you so much for taking on the role of the villain. Although we haven't given Judas very much to say, he is a "presence" in the room and at the table. During our research, we developed very sympathetic feelings for him. Judas was the only Judean in the group. Everyone else was from Galilee. This set him up from the beginning to feel just a little apart, a little isolated, an individual ripe for discontent. He had been a leathersmith prior to his association with Jesus. His role in the "family" was to handle the money. He apparently was very trusted by the group. He was loved by Jesus, who tried to hide his betrayal from the apostles by honoring him with the first sop at the Last Supper. If the others had known, they would never have let him leave. They would have killed him. There is an interesting theory that Judas was a violent Jewish nationalist. It is believed that his goal as a disciple was to mobilize the Jews to overthrow Rome. He believed that if Jesus was arrested, the people would be stirred up enough to do this. He supposedly did not know that Jesus would be killed, hence the small amount of money for turning him in. Thirty pieces of silver was approximately fourteen dollars, the average price of a slave. He sadly miscalculated everyone else's motives!

James and John: Along with his brother John, James was in a successful fishing business with their father. Peter and Andrew worked with them. James was one of the "Sons of Thunder" called that either because their father raised such a ruckus when they left the business to follow Jesus, or because of their somewhat violent tendencies. The brothers wanted to burn down a city because the people there wouldn't pay homage to Jesus! James was the more silent of the two brothers. He is intense and steadfast in his loyalty to Jesus. John was more vocal than his brother and was like most Galileans, a violent insurrectionist. He was every bit as loyal to Jesus as James, and was very likely the "beloved" disciple. James and John were part of the "inner circle" with Peter and Andrew.

Seating Chart for The Last Supper

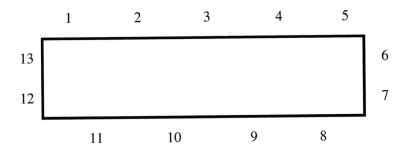

1. James
2. John
3. Jesus
4. Judas
5. Thomas
6. Philip
7. Bartholomew

8. Simon
9. James A.
10. Thaddeus
11. Matthew
12. Peter
13. Andrew